Black, Brown and Political

Get Informed, Get Empowered and Change The Game!

By: Chandra Brooks

Chandra Brooks
1009 E Capital Expwy
San Jose, CA 95121 #251
www.chandra-brooks.com

Publisher's Note: This is a work of fiction. Names, characters, places, and incidents are a product of the author's imagination. Locales and public names are sometimes used for atmospheric purposes. Any resemblance to actual people, living or dead, or to businesses, companies, events, institutions, or locales is completely coincidental.

Black, Brown and Political
ISBN-13: 978-1977986702
ISBN-10: 1977986706

TABLE OF CONTENT

Dedication

This book is dedicated to my husband, children and all my mentors and awesome public servants that have shown me how exemplary leaders can make significant positive change within our communities.

Introduction

Why I'm writing this book

Ten years ago, when I started following politics, I quickly figured out that it impacted everything. When I speak about local politics with friends, family, and acquaintances, they have no idea what I'm talking about. They vaguely know who their Mayor is or what he/she does or who their local elected officials were. They have no idea that in local elections they have the opportunity to vote in Judges, District Attorneys, and the Sheriff. This was alarming to me. Communities of color are affected the most by these elected leaders decisions, and we have no idea who they are, where they come from and if they would make fair decisions and policies that would be detrimental or beneficial to our community. I also realized that I only understood this by my years of work in the community, public and government relations.

It has to do with your makeup, the streets you drive on, your house payment, your rent, the clothes you buy, the car you drive. So why don't we know much about it? Is this on purpose? Or is it our fault? I think it could be a little bit of both.

As a community, we get excited about having a black President, a Latina Congresswoman or Senator but we forget about all the other elections going on all around us every day, like your local City Council elections, Board of Supervisors, Judges, and District Attorneys. But we'll stand in line for hours upon hours for newly released shoes, and phones without hesitation, while letting factors like weather, long lines and transportation prevent us from getting out the vote for a great candidate that would represent our community as a whole and our best interests.

I've also found that we are noticeably absent from the political arena when it comes to our money. For example, we'll spend money for tickets to sporting events, concerts and other forms of high ticket entertainment, but fail to make contributions to a grassroots community leader trying to raise money to run for office or even donate to campaigns that will benefit our communities.

It's clearly a priorities issue.

But how did we get here?

And more importantly, how do we correct it?

The answers to these questions are exactly why I wrote this book.

But to be clear, I am no political expert. I did not major in Political Science in College nor have I read countless books on this topic. My expertise comes from me being knee deep in the heart of movements that have gotten and continue to get results. And I want to share the knowledge I've gained from my experience to make politics and local government simple. I want it to ignite and empower people to get involved all the time and not just when they share something in common with a candidate like, age, race, color, etc. Or just a popular race.

My goal is to eliminate feelings of confusion and fear when it comes to politics and government, and let as many people as I can know that within each and every one of us lies the power to change things.

I'm not promising all the answers to every problem that we face as a society, but I can whole heartedly promise that within these pages you will find the NO BS, NO FLUFF tools and information needed to move you into action and to ignite the socially conscious human inside.

When I was a young teen, I was focused on boys, my looks and hanging out with friends. My focus was never the school, my future or anything political. I probably barely knew who the President of the United States was at the time.

Politics was not a daily topic in my household, school or my everyday life. I never understood the importance until I was an adult in my 30's and once I realized the significance, I was actually a little angry at my upbringing and education system for not educating us sooner- and when I say us- I mean People of Color.

Now let's rewind around 12 years back to when I became a teen mom. I'm sure it was not a surprise to my friends and family since school, and my future was definitely not a priority, and before becoming pregnant, I had been kicked out of three schools and walked across the graduation stage pregnant.

Matter of fact the same school district that expelled me from three schools my senior year of high school inducted me into their Hall of Fame in 2015 for my advocacy and activism work in the community. How ironic!

I've worked in community development, politics and social justice for the last 17 years. If I knew back then what I know now things for me would be so much different, but we all say that don't we.

If I were to talk to the 16-year-old Chandra, I would tell her...

Politics has to do with everything! It has to do with your makeup, your birth control, your roads, your homes, the clothes on your back, your opportunities, your freedoms, your religion and the list goes on.

Now, who makes these decisions that affect our everyday lives? Do you know? Do they look like you and me? More than likely they don't.

In 2017 a report from www.diversityinc.com reported 78% of Congress is White and 90% of the Senate is white as well. If you see the picture in the article, you can see a distinct image of who's running one of the most diverse countries in the world. Yes, you probably thought the President ran the country, right?! No, not by himself- the President must work with Congressional and Senate Representatives from every state. The President cannot make moves without the votes and consent of the House of Representatives and the Senate.

My point is we must engage in politics at the local level. Know your School Board Members, City Council Members, and Mayor, Board of Supervisors, Commissioners, State Senate and Assembly Members. These people are making decisions for you that affect your life every day. We must take our seats at the table or risk being on the menu! Do you get it? If we are not at the decision-making tables, we will continue to be on the Menu of life. Meanwhile, the leaders that look nothing like you, nor have been through the same life experiences as you, are making the decisions for you.

We've been letting this happen to us for centuries, and it must change. Although the number of people of color running for office and engaging in politics is increasing, it's not enough. We cannot leave it to Black Lives Matter, National Council of La Raza, NAACP and The Latino Victory Project and leaders like Maxine Waters, Jesse Jackson and Dolores Huerta to do all the fighting and advocacy for us. We must step up, get our voices heard, and get civically active in our communities NOW. We must identify young leaders in our communities and prepare them to run for political office, and WE MUST SUPPORT THEM. If we don't do this now, we will continue to have the same policies, laws and dim circumstances like housing, school loan debt, inequality and opportunity in the hands of the wealthy and privileged.

When I figured this out, I ensured I got civically active and quick. I would get to know and connect with all city, county, and state representatives and their staffers. I applied and was accepted into the Emerge California program, a Democratic Training program for women who want to run for political office. I started to educate my community and recruited other women to my commission and other commissions. I held a training called "Sit at the Table to be on the Menu," to teach communities of color to apply for boards and commissions and how to run for political office. In 2014, I was appointed as a Commissioner on the Status of Women and Girls for my county and in 2016 ran for California Democratic Party Delegate and won. These are just the small steps I decided to take and I'm sure my political career is not over. Only time will tell, but until then I will continue to advocate, support candidates that represent my values and will stand up for communities of color and not be afraid to challenge a system that was never created to serve us fairly.

Trust me, I know it's hard to try and trust a system that seems to never work out in our favor. Believe me it's tough, it's tough to stand up and continue to be defeated and defeated with no sign of change on the horizon. But I want to ask you how do you think the change is going to happen? Protest? Marching? Boycotting? No, this alone will not ensue change. We must infiltrate the system from the inside out along with all the tactics named above. Then, I promise you, we will see change.

Sit At the Table or Be On the Menu

Let me tell you what this means to me. This means that if we don't take our seats at decision-making tables, the people that don't look like us are going to be making decisions for us. Let me share a story. Every neighborhood has a school board. People get elected that live in that school district and they make decisions that affect the schools your children attend. Sometimes these are wonderful people that really care about kids and sometimes these are people who just want a title or a steppingstone to higher office. The people that just want the titles and the power usually stay on for a long time and how does this happen? Because nobody runs against them and they keep getting elected by you. Yes I said it. By YOU.

In a local school district not too far from me there is a contentious challenge happening on the school board. Several schools in this district do not have air conditioning but the air conditioning and certain upgrades for the schools have been approved (by the board) and the money has been allocated through a Measure on the ballot, that was passed by the voters, but even though the funds have been allocated none of the work has been completed. Yes the money has been approved for this work to be done and these air-conditioners to be installed but it's been a few years and the kids are still without air conditioning. But the contractors that the board approved to do the work continue to get paid while the kids go with no air conditioning. So when the good members of the board challenged the decision of this contractor some shady board members who are elected by the community, are totally dismissing the mishandling of this issue and the questions the superintendent and the good board members are trying to get cleared up in regards to the shady contractor. Wouldn't you be mad if you lived in the school district and your kids were in 100+ heat and these school board members keep twiddling their fingers and playing politics and games with the money that was allocated for this work? I hope this makes you angry! This is just an example of why we need to take our seats at the decision-making tables.

Now, what does this mean to you? To me it means we must take on leadership positions so others who may not have the same values or the best intentions are not the only ones making decisions for us. You see these elected leaders make decisions that affect us every day. So, we must prepare to take our seat at the table, or our opinions, values, beliefs, and desires will not be considered.

Where to start:

Usually, political leaders are local activists, community leaders, business owners and highly active community members that have been involved in their community for a long time. Usually, if a person comes out of the woodwork and runs for office, he/she is not successful because they have not made a name for themselves within their community or the community and the powers that be have not seen you put in the work.

So, my point is that you must establish yourself within your community first. Get involved in a cause that is important to you. Get to know your local elected officials; start to build some influence and network within your community. Join a board or commission within your city or county and start to do the work within the community. Join that neighborhood association and help build that playground, get the pot holes fixed, and get the street lights fixed. Clean up your neighborhoods. Show the community that you really care and that you're willing to do the work and you're not there for the title or glory.

Find out who the movers and the shakers are in the community and ask them to have coffee to introduce yourself. Tell them your interests and how you would like to get involved. You'll be surprised how resourceful they will be and how many doors may open. Do your research first to find out the "teams." Yes, I said, teams! "Teams" as in those who are on the Business side of Politics, who are on the Labor side of Politics, who are connected to "Influential Families". I'm telling you it can get complicated but the more you know, the better.

Then when election time comes, learn about the local leaders who are running in your city/town and do your research. Go to their campaign offices and get to know them, talk to their staff and tell them you would like to host a meet and greet at your house. Find what they stand for and ask them questions that are significant to you. Like schools, roads, why so many liquor stores are in your community and what he/she will do about it.

You will slowly figure out who to align yourself with and who are the people, candidates and local leaders who fight for all the right issues every day. These people need to become your friends and allies on the road to change.

<u>Let's see if you're ready to use your voice!</u>

Speak up and Take Your Seat at the Decision Making Tables. Go to **<u>https://quiz.leadquizzes.com/q/QhOBjd</u>** and take the quiz now!

2 Running For Office

So maybe you are an established businessman/woman, educator, pastor or some type of leader in your industry but not quite known in your community. Do all those things previously mentioned and then some. You must research what you would run for. Remember this tip: You can't just jump and run for Mayor. You need to start at a lower level and work your way up the political ladder. Usually, potential and aspiring candidates start at Commissioner, Delegate, School Board and City Council levels before running for Mayor or any higher level positions. If you try to jump right in and run for a high-level position without any real political experience, you will more than likely lose, especially in bigger cities, but in smaller more rural towns you may actually get lucky and have a good chance at winning.

I'd also suggest finding a political training program in your county, city or state. Google should be a good resource for that. At the end of this book, I'll provide some resources for that as well. I can say the best thing I ever did to prepare myself to run for office was the political training program for women called Emerge. They teach you how to fundraise, build influence, how to speak to the media, and how to run an effective campaign and much, much more. So, the moral of the story is, get your feet wet first, build some community influence and foundation, get some training and then consider running for office. Furthermore, have a strong moral compass that cannot be swayed by corporate interest or greed. If you (or a candidate) don't have a strong moral foundation, you can be easily influenced by hefty political contributions and favors by wealthy and influential people. If you are not ready to hold your ground and do the right thing, reconsider running. You must be strong enough to say No and democratic enough to understand that you may have to work with these same people in the very near future on a whole other issue. This is how politics works. You get over it and move on.

Another strong requirement is thick skin. You ever see those mailers and commercials during a political season that flood your mailbox and television? If you're like me and know most of the candidates on these mailers and commercials, you can definitely confirm that most of what they portray is lies, especially when they're just downright negative and ridiculous. The more ridiculous it sounds, the more than likely it's a huge exaggeration and a long stretch of the truth. So, you must be able to take the heat and still present yourself with integrity and poise while out in public, plus smile and be cordial with the opposition that put those lies out about you. It's a dog eat dog world, and they take no prisoners and only the strong survive.

I talked to several politicians within my community. I asked them what an aspiring political candidate should know before jumping into a race. Most of them said, to really understand the position, know the community well and the issues that are most important to the constituents. The problem that several aspiring politicians have is that they don't really know much about the position they're running for and the issues most important to their community, you would be surprised."

Why They Don't Want Us Active

I think you can figure this out for yourself, but if we are active and involved and at the decision-making tables then they lose their control, supremacy, and power. I honestly believe that it's set up that way and we just take the bait and fall for it. They don't teach us enough about the major systems that run our country; which are the Political, Judicial, and Education Systems. The Republican Party preps candidates from as early as high school to run for office starting at the School Board level by supporting, grooming and dumping money into their campaigns all the way to Congress. Don't believe me, do the research.

Our American systems are deep-rooted and founded on white supremacy and racist ideals. It was not made for us to be included. It was set up from the beginning for us to be subordinate. So, the only way we take it back is through education, overpowering and organizing at the grassroots level and bringing up our own groomed leaders. If we organized and developed this within our own communities, we could really create some significant change.

Imagine if we did the same thing white America does? What if we handpicked our own natural leaders in high school? Trained them up and supported their political careers intentionally. United and funded their campaigns, walked neighborhoods to get out the vote for them, volunteered on their campaigns to ensure they get elected. Think about it. Even leaders that may not be considered "young" that show interest in running and have the experience, platform and support to run a significantly strong campaign. What if we could unite, show up and support them in a real way? Unfortunately, as long as I have been involved in politics I have not seen the US, Black and Brown folks really get behind a candidate as we should.

You know who does?

The Asian communities.

If you are their candidate, trust me you will know. They will organize, give you money, walk precincts, volunteer on your campaign and have a fundraiser for you. Support like this usually leads to a successful campaign.

Take some good inventory and ask yourself; why don't we do the same? What do the Asian communities know, that we don't? I don't think they're smarter than us, stronger or more united. I believe we can learn something from the Asian communities. We must organize and unite as they do and stand united with candidates that will represent our interest. If we don't, we'll continue to have the same outcomes we are so angry about today.

Want to be proactive, talk to your local NAACP/Black leadership groups, La Raza and Latino-based community groups and start leading discussions on how to start identifying young leaders to prepare them to run for office. Ask them what we are doing as a community to identify, recruit and nurture our next generation of leadership. If they can't communicate a plan, start your own. Start a political action group in your community that recruits and trains potential candidates to not only be potential political candidates but potential community leaders. What I learned in life is that we must not wait for people to give us opportunities, we must create them. If we wait on people to open doors or give us permission, we might be waiting forever.

4 Easy To Understand Local Government Structure

I truly believe that we don't know what we don't know. Nobody taught us about neighborhood associations, School Boards, City Councils and Board of Supervisors. I also didn't know anything about city and county commissions that advised the decision-makers on issues within my community. I only found out this information because I was around the right people. What about the everyday people that go to work every day and come home raising their families taking the kids to sports activities paying their taxes and their bills on time but want to get involved but just don't know where or how to start.

Before you start aspiring for these high level positions like Mayor, State Senator or Assemblywoman you must get your feet wet and get some experience at the grassroots level. Don't get me wrong there have been people, mostly celebrities and very wealthy individuals, who have ran for political office at higher levels for the first time ever and have won. Of course this is very rare and you must be very rich. The following are local and grassroots opportunities that you should get involved in if you're interested in really changing your community, schools and the world we live in to start navigating your way to a life of servant leadership.

(This may seem easier said than done, but I'm living proof that it's possible. If you have questions or need additional resources reach out to me at Chandra@chandra-brooks.com)

Neighborhood Associations

Like I have mentioned before and in all my videos, local government decisions affect you faster and more directly than the National Political decisions. For example, we all have neighborhood associations. These neighborhood associations are usually assembled and supported by your local city council office and staff. So, if you're upset about the city street lights, speed bumps, garbage, crime or any other neighborhood issue, it would be a brilliant move to get involved in your local neighborhood associations. The more leadership you have there, the more likely you can get things done for you and your neighbors. Meetings are usually once a month and named after whatever your neighborhood or area name is, for example. If your neighborhood is "Point Blank Community" the neighborhood association name is probably Point Blank Neighborhood Association. Get Active!

School Boards

The next important local government structure you should pay attention to is your school boards. Do you know who the members are of the schools your kids attend? Have you attended their meetings and did you know you elected them? These folks make the financial, resource, and policy decisions for your kids' school district. You should be attending, engaged and an outspoken voice on the decisions being made by the elected school board members. It's important to know who we are electing into these roles. Most are great people, but some are just using this stepping stone for their political career. I'd also recommend that you think about running for school board in your area. The elections and process are not too hard and not as competitive as city council and the higher positions within the city. This is your first step.

City & County Commissions

City and County Commissions are an advisory leg of the city and county government, and they advise the city council and/or Board of Supervisors on issues within the city and county. Below are the usual names of city and county commissions:

- Planning Commission

- Parks and Recreation Commission

- Arts Commission

- Senior Commission

- Housing Commission

- Status of Women's Commission

- Human Relations Commission

These are the basic commission every city manages. If any of these issues interest you, you can apply for these commissions online and work your connections and networking skills to get appointed. Yes, remember it's not about what you know - but who you know.

I've sat on the Commission on the Status of Women and Girls for the last three years, and it's been wonderful. We influence policy on equal pay, equal rights for women, we advocate for women in the county jail system and provide funding and support to women organizations and programs throughout the county.

Some may say that sitting on a commission is a stepping stone to higher political office. I can confirm and deny that claim. Many commissioners move onto higher office while several serve and never move on.

City Council or City Representatives

Every city may have a particular name for their city representatives. Some call them district representatives, city council members, and sometimes but rarely Alderman. These are elected city officials that make decisions for the city. Most of these decisions have to do with city planning, parks and recreation, city programs, city housing, homelessness, rent control, streets, and neighborhoods, everything in your city. They have a certain number of representatives depending on the number of citizens plus one Mayor. The City Council is the extension of the Mayor and work directly with him/her representing their area of the city. Like I mentioned each Council member represents a certain portion of their city, this must be the area they reside in. If you choose to run for this office you must reside in the area you would like to run in. You can't live in one area of the city and run for another. For example, if you live in District 2 of your city, you cannot run for District 6 city council.

The city council members have a tough job because they have to appease every citizen within their jurisdiction, including some with louder voices than others. You know how they say the squeaky wheel gets the oil, right. It's true, the louder, more engaged and involved you are in your local issues , know how to work the system, who the main players are and how to get things done, your concerns and issues will probably be addressed faster. This is another example of people power and a reminder that these leaders work for us and are sworn into work for the people, not for their own benefit.

Do you know the people who are usually the most active and the loudest getting their voices heard? NOT people of color! These people are at all the neighborhood meetings, City council meetings and special Town halls to address issues. Why don't we show up to these events?

There could be several reasons why.

1. We are not on their email list or we are not the audience they target.

2. It's not interesting enough or the football game is on that night or we're just too tired after   work.

3. We don't trust politicians or the system.

4. We don't know the importance of the meetings.

These people are pretty tired as well but they know the importance of their voice and if they raise it loud enough the leaders will pay attention. We must do better!

County Board of Supervisors

A board of supervisors is a governing body that oversees the operation of county government in all U.S. counties in Arizona, California, Iowa, Mississippi, Virginia, and Wisconsin as well as 16 counties in New York. Similar to a city council, a board of supervisors has legislative, executive, and quasi-judicial powers.

The county Supervisors supervise the Sheriff and usually the County Jail, probation departments, and county appointed officers. They have monthly meetings that are open to the public and have opportunities for people to make public comment. Do your research and attend one of your Board of Supervisor meetings to see what's going on.

These elected officials make decisions on transportation and jails. They are an administrative division of the state. So basically, they implement and refine state law within the county, whereas the city implements and produces their own laws and public policy.

5 Change Starts with You

You know that person on Facebook and Social Media sites who complains about politicians? Or are you that one family member that likes to talk about politics and watch TV but you're not active in your community to work on the issues that upset you. Are you also upset about what the politicians are not doing and you know exactly what they should do? I hope that's not you, but if it is, listen up.

You obviously have a strong opinion and are very observant about what's going on in the world around you.

You want change to happen, but it's so much easier to make a post and complain than to really do something about the problem. Right?

No- Wrong! The Change starts with you. We must infiltrate the system if we want to change it. We also must use our voice, influence, and power to enforce and encourage the change we want to see. Don't be that person I just described, leave a legacy for your children to be proud of and say, "My mom/dad stood up for something, and they made a difference in this world." WE must lead by example.

The system was never set up for us or to serve us. We must be the action takers, risk takers, and activists. We need to teach ourselves the works of the government and how we can affect and change policy and systems that affect us every day. How are we going to fix these issues if we are not at the decision-making table? Like I mentioned before, sit at the table or be on the menu. If you're not interested in running for office at least learn the system and learn how to navigate the systems in order to get it to work for you and your community. For example, I have a mentor that is a former Black Panther. He is not an elected official, but his power and influence affect many decisions within the community. He pays attention to what's going on within the community so he can address his concerns or confront elected officials directly so they can make the right decisions and he holds them accountable. They listen to him because they know if they don't, he can affect their future political career or he will be a pain in their side until they do, plus they highly respect his opinion. He also has an influence on ensuring Black and Brown qualified individuals are provided the same high-level opportunities as everyone else. This is why it's so important we build, develop, and get involved and active within our community. His influence didn't happen overnight; his influence developed over time and consistent leadership within communities of color. You must also not be intimidated by elected officials and understand they put their pants on just like you and me. This only happens with involvement and engagement within your community and a consistent track record of getting things done.

6 Why It Always Comes Back To Policy

Let me tell you how I even got involved in politics and why. I worked in nonprofit and community organizations for a long time and always had the passion to help others. I learned how to manage teams, raise money, work with the Board of Directors and create real programs that helped teen moms, low income families, and young people who needed a second chance. These are the many skills that I've learned working in the nonprofit sector. Although I enjoyed this and it was very fulfilling, I realized that this work was just a Band-

Aid. Yes I can continue to help teen moms and at risk youth but what is the real solution to this problem? I realized I didn't just want to Band-Aid issues, I wanted to create solutions and these issues were socioeconomic problems. Socioeconomic problems had to be addressed and solved at the policy level.

What is a policy? A policy is a course or principle of action adopted or proposed by a government, party, business, or individual. Policy controls everything and having the right elected official that vote and create this policy is even more important. It affects your children's schools, the money they get for education, the pot holes in the streets, the taxes you pay at the store, your rent, mortgage and even the type of gas available and its prices. Oh, and your food. Have you payed close attention to how many fast food restaurants and liquor stores are in your neighborhood?

As taxpayers, we have a stake in affecting public policy and the overall structure and power of our government. Understanding policy gives us the power to influence and problem-solve the issues that affect our community. What people don't realize and/or know is laws and policies can be changed, but the only way for them to change is through electing the right people into office that will work with all people and for all people. Also having strong community leaders that hold these elected officials accountable to recreate, revise, and implement a new policy that is more beneficial to the community it's being enforced within.

Have you ever heard someone say, why don't they just change that rule? Or that's a stupid rule; someone needs to change that, it doesn't make sense. Someone makes those rules and just like with any company, you have policies. This is the same way to look at a city or county. It's run just like a business. Every company has policies, right? And who makes those policies? The CEO, President, Board of Directors of the company or organization - The decision makers, create, draft, review, and vote on the policies they feel are necessary and the ones that are initiated by community leaders and advocates. If you're not involved, you have absolutely no say in the process, and a policy will get implemented without your input or knowledge. This happens to us every day.

7 Run Women Run

The number of women in elected office is significantly low compared to the number of seats available. Women that hold seats in Congress are under 20% of the over 500 seats in the House of Representatives. This is unfortunate and something we should really start nurturing in our communities. Imagine significant women of color in positions of power. What would that look like for our kids and grandkids and their future? These women are the backbones of our families. They are the nurturers, disciplinarians, providers, risk takers, problem solvers, collaborators, and peacemakers. Imagine that!

They do say that when women lead, things are more just, fair, and collaborative. Unfortunately, women and more specifically women of color have been consciously and unconsciously excluded from and severely underrepresented in politics. Can you see how this can affect what is going on in the world today? Now more than ever the world needs our leadership and perspective. You have old white men making decisions about women's bodies and healthcare. White men are deciding who is allowed to come into this country and who should be excluded. Sexual orientation of individuals is now a target and threat to the safety of our country. Would this happen if we had women and more specifically women of color in decision-making offices?

Fortunately, now more than ever there are organizations that are willing to get behind women to run for office. In the midst of the last election and following the Women's March (which I had some issues with) women are interested in stepping into more leadership roles and the following organizations will help women run and win. These organizations will teach women how to manage a campaign, fundraise, and run a successful campaign. In the past, it may have seemed like a far-fetched idea or unrealistic pipe dream, but today, the country is ready for a new type of leadership style, and it will take women to show us how it's done. Below are some Political Training programs for women:

Emerge California

Emerge California is a political training program for Democratic women. I've been through this program and it was one of the best decisions of my life. In this program you learn the skills you need to run a successful campaign and become a strong candidate. After you go through the program you are provided resources and connected to a huge network of women that can help you run and win. The Emerge program has a 70% win rate, meaning 70% of graduates run for office and win. There are also several emerge programs throughout the country.

Emily's List

EMILY's List's vision is to be a driving force of change in America. By electing more pro-choice Democratic women to national, state and local office, EMILY's List will consistently infuse our government with leaders who will drive change; Change that truly matters today, tomorrow and forever.

She Should Run

Our Ask a Woman to Run tool provides a way for individuals to tell us about great women leaders they know who should consider a run for office. Our first-of-its-kind She Should Run Incubator offers resources and a community that meets women where they are in their paths to elected leadership. We listen to our members and work with them to overcome roadblocks that prevent them from running for office.

VoteRunLead

VoteRunLead supports the aspirations of women who want to transform our country and democracy through their participation as leaders.

Furthermore, think about how this will motivate and inspire our young ladies. To see women in powerful government positions will hopefully ignite and motivate other young women to look towards politics as a career possibility.

8 A Call to Action

If we continue to wait for the next person to make a move and take action, we will continue to wait forever. If you are reading this book, you already have some interest and conviction to get active. You are never too young or never too old to start doing something. Stop worrying about what people think, say or feel when you start taking action. Something is better than nothing, but it must be effective and with the best intentions. Our communities need your leadership, your activism, and your voice.

Standing on the sidelines hoping for change is not enough anymore. It is clear as water that this is detrimental to our communities. Our people are being passed over for jobs they are over qualified for, they're being killed by untrained and biased police officers, and voting laws are being implemented that make it harder for us to vote every year. Our kids are being discriminated against in the classroom because the school board has not addressed any discriminatory policies that will protect our children. Effective teachers of color are being fired and passed up for jobs because someone feels threatened by their presence and skin tone. Our children will continue to be suspended and expelled from school, arrested on campus for small infractions because the school administration and board feel it's safer to have police on campus not realizing the consequences and outcomes that will arise having officers take over discipline in the school.

Women of color will continue to get paid .50 cents to the man's dollar and overlooked for leadership roles because we have no representation at the decision-making table looking out for our best interest. These are the realities we will continue to face if we don't step up and create a place for our voices today. If we don't start working together as people of color to identify leaders that will be recognized by the people and work for the people we will continue to complain without much to show for it.

We are better, stronger, and smarter than that.

How will you implement everything that you learned in this book? How will you take action in your local community and stop being part of the problem and part of the solution? Remember it starts with you! Things you can start doing today:

1. Research your local elected officials

2. Start following them on social media

3. Attend a city council or board of supervisor meeting

4. Apply for a city or county commission, find the commission of your interest and attend a meeting

5. Attend your neighborhood association meetings

6. Look up and meet with your local school board members and find out the issues within your kid's school

7. During election season, find out who is running for office locally and do your research on them. Attend a meet and greet and find a candidate that represents your best interest. If you like them, and they seem like a strong candidate you can support, walk precincts for them, and donate to their campaign, they need you!

Do it for your future, your kid's future and all the young people coming behind you. We need you! The time is now!

ABOUT THE AUTHOR

Chandra is the former Vice President of the National
Association for the Advancement of Colored People
(NAACP), Executive Director of Building Peaceful Families,
Co-Founder of Women Get it Done Silicon Valley and
graduate of Emerge California, a political training program
for Democratic Women and holds a Bachelor's Degree in
Business Management.

She is an appointed Commissioner of Santa Clara County's
Commission on the Status of Women and Girls and Co-Chair

of the Crime and Violence Committee that manages the Commissions oversight of Elmwood's Women's correctional facility and most recently elected as a delegate to the California Democratic Party.

In 2013 Chandra received the Portrait of Success Award from the Hispanic Development Corporation and in 2014 the Activist of the Year Award from Latinos Action Media (LAM). In 2015 Chandra was named one of the Most Influential Women in Silicon Valley from The Silicon Valley Business Journal and inducted into the East Side Unified High School District Hall of Fame; and in 2016 named Women of the Year from 100 Black Women of Silicon Valley an Latina with Vision Award from New York Life. Then in 2017 received the Leadership Award from The California League of United Latin American Citizens.

In 2017 Chandra Launched The SocialPreneur, a purpose driven business that prepares potential candidates to get ready to run for political office and mentors women to own their power and leadership within their company, business, and/or community.

Since the launch of The SocialPrenuer Chandra has been featured in the Huffington Post, Modern Latina Magazine and dozens of online web shows and podcast highlighting the message of Civic Engagement and Women in Leadership.

STAY CONNECTED

To learn more about how Chandra can help you show up and change the game, go to her website:
http://www.chandra-brooks.com

For the latest information on live sessions, speaking engagements and conferences that can help you be the leader you were meant to be, connect on FaceBook
https://www.facebook.com/empoweringcommunities4u

Have questions, need support or guidance, and to request one on one sessions For access to training, Chandra@chandra-brooks.com

Made in the USA
Las Vegas, NV
28 September 2021

31294823R00036